CITY OF PALACES

Para Isaac Berliner,
Diego Rivera. 1934

City of Palaces

Poems by ISAAC BERLINER

Drawings by DIEGO RIVERA

✳

JACOBY PRESS

1996

TRANSLATED BY MINDY RINKEWICH

JACOBY PRESS

25 Dexter Drive North

Basking Ridge, NJ 07920

ISBN 0–9649634–0–X

To my dear children,
Amalia & David

★

TABLE OF CONTENTS

✶

Isaac Berliner and Diego Rivera. Mexico City, 1934.

FOREWORD

$\mathcal{M}$ore than sixty years ago the poet Isaac Berliner and the artist Diego Rivera collaborated on a volume of illustrated poems. The title page of the collection, entitled *La Cuidad de los Palacios* (The City of Palaces) reads, "Isaac Berliner and Diego Rivera 1936." We hold in our hands a new edition of that rare collaboration which reproduces Diego Rivera's original illustrations to Isaac Berliner's poems. The poems, originally printed in Yiddish, have been translated into English making them accessible to a wider audience.

Isaac Berliner, born in Lodz, Poland in 1899, arrived in Texcoco, Mexico in 1921 and sold images of saints for a living. He wanted to participate fully in the culture. To become less distinguishable from the men around him and to get to know the Mexicans better, he let his mustache grow. The thousands of impressions he collected became poems published in Yiddish by the leading Jewish newspaper, *Der Veg* (The Way). His poetry was well received by its Yiddish-speaking readers. Yiddish is a fusion language combining the elements of its Romance, Hebrew, Aramaic, Germanic and Slavic components, and is printed in Hebrew characters.

Diego Rivera, the muralist, painter, and artist, was well-known for his sensitivity toward issues of social justice. Through word of mouth, Rivera learned of Isaac Berliner's interest in Mexico and his contributions to *Der Veg*. The artist sent for the poet, and a bond of friendship was formed. They would get together on Sundays. The topics were always political affairs, the poverty of Mexico and its social contrasts. Sometimes they are joined by Frida Kahlo, Rivera's wife and a well-known artist in her own right.

One day the idea was born to collaborate on a book. *La Ciu-*

· *xi* ·

dad de los Palacios would be created with Berliner's words and Rivera's illustrations. It would be the subject of their Sunday encounters and aimless wanderings through the streets of Mexico City; the fruit of their unconditional friendship and their passion for art and social justice.

Although Berliner was aware of Mexico's palatial architecture and natural scenic beauty, he spoke of them only as points of contrast. His selective gaze fixed only on the naturally sad. *The City of Palaces* was transformed into a cold, ungiving mother, uninterested in her children thirsting for a gulp of milk. In overpopulated Mexico City, the abundance of flowers and fruits disappeared from many tables. Tortilla makers, who made the daily bread of Mexico since time immemorial, survived on meager fare. Berliner identified with the unfortunate of his adoptive mother country; he, too, was a pariah. He was a Jew, a marked being, born of stigma, a displaced child in the city which neglected its children.

Berliner, with the strong support and encouragement of his wife, Consuelo, went on to publish four more books of poetry and receive international acclaim. Master Diego Rivera had few peers.

I visited the Berliners in Mexico in the late 1930s, and have vivid memories of evenings spent listening to Isaac Berliner read his poetry in his naturally rich deep voice. A chance meeting with the poet's son, Dr. David Berliner, at a family wedding reception, prompted him to sponsor this translation project.

Throughout their long relationship Isaac Berliner and Diego Rivera were good friends and, coincidentally, both died in the same year, 1957.

Harry Jacoby

CITY OF PALACES

ON THIS SIDE OF THE OCEAN

On this side of the ocean
the earth glows under a sunny flame
in eternal summer green.
Years pass—Going where—
at a calm slow pace,
like lazy tired little donkeys,
like the quiet drawn out singing
of a sad village song—
and in the heart a strong desire
pulsating rocking rocking
like a fly in a spider's web.

On this side of the ocean
there are broad fields too,
Every firmly packed stalk
under a hail of tropical fire
awaiting the sickle's clang
Then, storage under lock and key,
in barns bursting with abundance.
And in the cities, by day and by night,—
the unspoken beseeching in the cries of children,
people fainting from hunger.

On this side of the ocean
life leads us along step by step
in the quiet passing of days
to a distant misty road—
and every step, that it takes,
crushes a dream underfoot ...

and eternal, sun-drenched time
keeps right on marching along the middle of the road
weaving a chain of dead dreams
wandering around, crawling along, –
dragging a heavy chain in its wake.

On this side of the ocean
Poison flows freely
in broken homes strangled by
bitter poverty, who has moved in.
A darkness inhabits the thresholds,
although the bright sun scatters
her red golden beads everywhere –
These rays are hard and stingy;
They gild the hill of stone,
but poison flows from molten steel
for the people languishing in the valley.

On this side of the ocean
a body in pants is a man,
revenge is the strongest desire,
a bread knife – a weapon . . .
In the hills, in the valleys and fields
a man's life isn't worth a damn
People live as they breathe by the day.
The next day is uncertain and bleak
Conscience is a superfluous plague.
in the grey blind chase –
Men's souls rot in the garbage.

On this side of the ocean
I have struck deep roots;

though my home is a distant strange land
I am wrapped in a sun-woven weave,
I feel comfortable with the shirt on my back,
I feel comfortable with the life that I lead . . .
Like an eagle in flight, on the hunt
speeding over giant mountains,
I too fly and I soar
bearing bright days with me
to gild the song that I sing.

*R*uins of temples
remind us
of the stride
and the swagger
of warriors on horses–
armored brutes,
who made
Indian blood flow
like rain,
who fertilized generous fields–
And Jesus on high
in his heavenly palace,
sent a bloody smile
through the smoke of the canon
to his crazed penitents and his servants,
who greedily nourished themselves
with the dried blood on the crosses.

Ruins of churches
remind us;–
of the holy Virgin
on thrones
of heavenly incest,
lit with love;
by people who lay
with red-hot wounds,
like sheep to the slaughter,
in the cold dark caves
of the church,
tied up

like sheaves–

The holes and cracks of the churches
that tell
of the dying of martyrs–
Indian ruins remind us:–
of cyclones,
that scattered
the peace and the faith of the Aztecs
like dust,
of women, of men and of children
in shackles
for the atonement
of nobody's sins–

And swords of iron and steel,
that cut up the bodies
of men and of women and children;–
and priests–
Those godly protectors–
who cut up their peace and their years
amid holy whispers,
like reapers
in fields reaping corn.

It's still around,
You can still feel the glow
of the sacred fury
of Spaniards –

Ruins of temples
remind us; –
how bloody
the Indian earth is.

CITY OF MUDPUDDLES

City of mudpuddles the size of rivers,
Tattered walls on low built shacks
Your grey, hungry people sneaking around on sidewalks
wrapped in rags.

And little children cry, grow pale and shudder,
lying around in stinking yards–
City, how I would like to run from you,
leaving no traces of my heavy steps.

So many generations have walked upon your body,
and you've grown even more cruel, ugly and black–
with poverty dancing through your crooked streets.

You've scattered pain on every wall here,
brought disaster upon forlorn homes

by now–there's a struggling victim in every one.

IT'S FREE

*I*t's free—
The glow
of sunlight on rags,
that hang from weary bodies
in filthy tatters
the right to stretch your limbs out
like a lonely dog beside the fence—

It's free
The dream of bread
and flowers,
of fields and trees and twigs;
Its free
to keep your mouth shut
when you feel the screams begin to rise.

The desolation creeping out of houses,—
a blind shadow—
leaving behind
the crying of children,
the sorrow of mother's,
the fathers' helpless worry
and long, dark moments—
The road to joy fenced off—

So what?—
The hunger that dries the blood,
is free—

DESIERTO DE LOS LEONES

*O*ut of the ruins of the old convent,
out of the earth, out of iron and stone,
I still hear the stifled cries,
the bitter wailing that comes
out of every corner and crack
crawling along the walls ...

I seem to see an old capuchin monk
out of the old convent –
spreading his hands like a spider
and his scornful lips whisper;
"A man has profaned God" –

A man has been burned

Out of the cracks of the old convent –
The voice of a priest at prayer –
"The love of women – is sin –
Oh, God – man is so small" –

The priests themselves
violated those sinful bodies –

Out of the ruins of the old convent,
a shudder, a rustle, a call; –
"The body torn apart with pliers,
hands ripped from the trunk,
The children, the sister, the wife,
hands and feet cut up.
Bodies shackled in chains,
racked limb by limb,

Water dripping drop by drop,
boring holes in their heads" –

You can hear the walls whisper to this day
in the caves of the old convent –

TEOTIHUACAN

*Y*ou thousand year old Pyramids in your stony silence
among the silent flatlands and the hills, –
How many prayers, how many mystic praises
did a people at peace sing to you? –

I have absorbed your silence
I only know that centuries ago
a people removed from other peoples
sang the praises of unknown gods.

Perhaps you have the steps of my great great grandfather
    upon you
and my blood bears the heritage of a secret from afar, –
Do my origins lie buried beneath your stones
in their endless, timeless silence? –

Who were those marvelous giants, those strong men,
who laid the granite and the heavy stones? –
Older peoples have given birth to new ones,
Only the pyramids remain unchanged

You pyramids –
Were your builders Egyptians,
Phoenicians,
Jews, perhaps? –

I know, the holy Christian faith
of the Spanish Inquisition
besmirched Toltek's name
to scare the whole world with wild indian stories,
to rob
the quiet peace,

to erase
these nations from the earth—

Sun over the pyramids—
covering the eternal secret with your flames—
Out of the ruins of the old convent
shadows crawl—
A mass of thousands all told—
Body follows body, like a snake—

Heads, feet, hands
move separately—

POPOCATEPETL

*P*opo–
Body hardened to stone with fleece of snow,–
thousands of years scream from your body
in a silent scream–

At rose-blue dawn
the sun drapes your white head
in multicolored stripes
like ribbons.

Winds–
invisible monsters riding at a gallop–
dashing about upon you, howling as they plunder,–
whistling and singing the songs of faraway lands.

How many secrets
accumulated in the rush of generations
lie hidden in your depths?–
How many marks
recorded in blood
on every single stone?–

Popo, I want you to carry me on your body
like a stone,
Would you reveal
your wonders to my silence–

Popo–
Mysterious white giant–
The sun, threw a spear at you
in the dark moments toward evening,
all lit up–

Now I see,
long vanished generations
bleeding
from your spinal cord—

How many wanderers have trod on your white skin?—
How many glowing steps?—

Death
is pacing about at your ankles—
This cold, white wonder
blooming
on your back—

*Y*ou like to stop and look at the moldering carved doors
of shabby buildings, built centuries ago,
at every carving and stone sculpture of old monasteries, –
and every crack in the splitting walls tells you so many secrets.

You hold every head of stone dear, every manuscript, you love
  their shadows,
You like to fondle and cherish every bit of hieroglyphic.
From every stone the old primative tribes mutely sing
long forgotten symphonies more beautiful than Beethoven's Ninth.

You gaze upon them with such pleasure, you seem so close to
  everything here . . .
and the unknown joy, grief and fear of alien grandfathers is
  also yours;
Along paths overgrown with grass, Cuatemoc of the feathered head,
  the last hero of the Aztecs,
tells you tales of such bravery and such sacrifice.

And you imagine that you still can see the wild, glowing tongues
  of flame
upon the brown skin of the King's feet; armor clad
  shapes materialize;
Hernon Cortez, his flashing eyes driven by gold greed,
screams his commands at the victim; Tell me where you hid the
  gold you dog? –

And Huitzilopochtli – God of war – nourished by human blood,
Mute stone head – dull hard stare –
No longer can he still his hunger with the dripping blood and
  fluttering hearts in the stone pipes,

as he did in those crude times when one tribe savagely
    crushed another.

Anahuak is big and every idol has given you a sign,
The origins of all the tribes from the Navahos to the Mayans is
    not unknown to you—
I too would like to learn the secret of peace through the search
    for lost generations as you have,
not following those lost thousands of years as the bereaved
    follow funerals.

Are there others like you, quiet temperaments,
who collect little stones and pick up gems from vanished one upon
    a times?—
You have locked yourself in a temple of forgotten cultures
like a sunbeam lowering itself through the cracks of
    black valleys.

For you every shard of an old grey pot
is a holy talisman left by peoples of bygone days—
If only you could, you would hide from the world of today
and go back to the secret, distant past; body and soul.—

You are in touch with every little bit of something along these
    strange roads,
Bits of the heritage—moldy little stones, old monasteries—
Your childhood didn't come into being upon these flaming prairies
You've been seduced by wanderlust like me and like the others.

Anahuac—The name the conquerers used in Mexico.
Huitzilopochtli—A god to whom the Aztecs made human sacrifices.

CONTRASTS

City of palaces, you stone box,
surrounded by a hilly chain in the valley.
Your guts are full of the wildest of contrasts,
of misery, hunger and the joy of abundance.

Your asphalt streets are full of the rush
of speeding cars and trolleys;
but you also have back streets like piles of garbage,
where the day lies around in rags.

Your insides contain churches and convents
The houses are built of marble and stone;
There are people like worms on small dusty streets,
in little clay hovels – in holes of filth . . .

The little shacks there are built of clay bricks
covered with rusty tin roofs, –
A string and a rag – is a cradle for children . . .
shirts covering bodies – a sack in shreds –

In stone palaces behind locks of iron,
silk clings to female bodies, –
The wine that they drink is drawn from barrels
Their day to day joy bursts into drunken dancing.

On dirty little steps, next to brown containers,
The silk on their bodies – the glow of the sun;
Their wine is pulke – in little clay pots –
They drink down their poverty, warming their blood . . .

Oh, city of palaces, you carrier of misery! –
The weight on your shoulders has increased . . .
You have people, who sleep on soft beds and still more
asleep on the filthy ground . . .

pulke– A specifically Mexican alcoholic beverage.

HOMES

*I*n homes where poverty has taken hold like a leech
and stares out of the walls with bleak horror—
and countless people in those holes crawl around like moths
moldering boards—that have devoured their own lives—

And it seems that someone here has shaped clay figures,
that lie around in the streets—ruins made of earth—
The spiders lead a home life on these walls too,
Only the abject human being can't hide his shame from
    the streets . . .

Go tell it to the great wide world, go tell it
A dog in his kennel has it better than a man
A deathbed confession isn't worth making,
and people just can't sink any lower . . .

Why tell the whole world about it, why tell the world?—
The cave man had it better in his hills and caves . . .

*I*n the dirty little city streets–
In the echo of clamor and noise
There are children lying around, whom no one cares for,
children longing for a little milk.

In the dirty little city streets–
In hovels of garbage and clay,
there are mothers on their own
with dried, sickly breasts.

In the dirty little city streets
Hunger lurks at every step–
And out on the fields there's so much
food to eat–gifts of God

On the dirty little city streets
people, whom people scorn
lie on paper, on mats of straw,
huddled in the dusty grey.

In the dirty little city streets
misery built his palace,–
In the little houses of tin and wire
there's a dream of bread floating around.

CROOKED STREETS

Crooked little streets, black pavements full of holes,
Tiny, low little Lilliputan houses.
Doors, doors – black little holes as though mice lived there.
sticking out gloomily into the street and staring.

Feet crawl and dirty bodies bow,
Brown faces with grinding teeth
looking for a meal on the grey stones.
And they appear from everywhere like ants.

In mute smiling sadness,
they look for a tortilla somewhere on the sidewalks
or at the stone thresholds of every gate.

Haughty passersby stare with cold arrogance
At the huddled man on lonely boulevards
with his dry throat and languishing desire.

COURTYARDS

*D*ays lie around–in the long, narrow courtyards like TB victims
    spitting out their lungs ...
Poverty has spread dark spots on the heated walls like measles on
    a skinny body ...
Dogs lie with their spines pressed to the earth, their little
    feet high in the air, waiting
for buzzing flies that fall on their noses and their
    babbling tongues.

There are fat, brown women sitting beside stone barrels, rubbing
    dirty laundry and panting.
Next to door–that are holes in the wall–beans in brown clay
    pots roast on tin heaters.
The thin fingers of white-haired old women go through the hair on
    children's heads.
Men lie stretched on the damp earth next to the dirty
    thresholds, snoring.

Children, wearing tattered pants on their bare bodies, like bits
    of rags for patching–
jump around screaming happily in sick courtyards full of poverty
    and horror,
with sparkling eyes like bits of shining coal in brown
    clay balls.

A daughter, with painted lips and eyebrows, guides her old brown
    father into the house,
staggering like a wooden doll, in a wet blouse that looks as
    though it's been dipped in mud,
cursing him for drinking up their last fifty cents at the saloon.

BAKERY

*A*n open door between two tattered walls,
an open door, sticking out into the swarming grey street corner—
Inside—the brown hands of seven women
kneading corn tortillas—the daily bread.

Seven women standing—like stone and copper idols—
Their faces full of wrinkles like a carved zigzag pattern.
Singing sad songs to a clapping rhythm.
A child lying on the ground, wrapped in rags, helps them with
    their wailing—

In the middle of the room—a square oven of grey clay
on it—a black tin plate heated to glowing red.
Seven standing women have been provided, no home or bed of
    their own,
who spend their days baking bread for others, to the tune of
    sad songs.

ON THE HARD STONE

*I*n an old, grey and tattered
soldier's coat,
wrapped around his dirty, naked body, there's a man—
half of him lying on the sidewalk, half in the gutter,
amid the daily screaming and the children's cries.

There's a man lying with his head on the hard stone,
with two eyes—
black-sparkling bits of glass
with a fearful empty stare—

There's a man propped up against the hard stones—
with a sparse little beard of scattered hairs sticking out
a little hill covered with fall grass—
and well-hidden smiles repose upon
his face
in resentful wrinkles—
saliva flowing from his mouth
like liquid from split
coconuts—

MARIJUANA

*T*he road is so muddy–
There is a man shuffling along
His lazy steps tread on the damp earth
as though his feet were heavy weights–
and eyes, that gleam like candles,
spreading the flames that fall
on female bodies and hips,
on the tender faces of girls–

That's that–
He can't take his eyes off them–
Why would anyone want to
quench the flame of passion
in his own eyes?–

He smokes marijuana–
A drug–

As he walks on the dream becomes real,–
The ground isn't muddy–
He's walking on carpets,
caressing his feet as he walks;
He can't hear the moaning and begging
of children on dirty street corners,–
Thousands of singers are singing–
Quartets making music–

Is somebody fainting from hunger?–
Are there outstretched hands that implore?–
Are there faces with skin going dry?–

There is nobody fainting from hunger.

There are no outstretched hands that implore
No faces with skin going dry.–
He's a young emperor
on thrones of red bleeding light–
It's nirvana–

He smokes marijuana–
A drug–
He's walking on carpets–
on muddy ground–

VAGABONDS

*V*agabonds–
scorned by man
and God–
Who prepared you
for the wounds and torment
of the city? . . .

Vagabonds–
rags
on your burning bodies,
fatherless,
childless, wifeless–
Who lit the glow in your eyes? . . .

Vagabonds–
There is a dark secret
in your flaming eyes . . .
Who drained the joy from you;
whom were they doing a favor?

Vagabonds–
The city has bound you
to the altar of poverty.

A BASTARD

*W*hen you were born, my child of the filth,
Misery was already clasping you to his breast,
and dogs bewailed your fate
beside dilapidated shacks, beside grey fences.

When you were born the sun hid
all its bright lights, and it was night
when you were born; and so a black destiny
will stalk you all your years on this cold earth.

No one caressed you in your cradle of rags,
and no nanny raised you,–
Your fate gave shape to itself
among the rusty tin, earth and bricks there.

Your lips suckled no mother's milk,
No mother's breasts cuddled you;
A prostitute in her misery, or the lowest kind of bitch
left you here on this grey garbage–

*W*here are the mothers,
who left
their children to rot
on dark street corners
The children,
who carry
a hidden
curse in the depths of their hearts? –

Where are the mothers,
who set the blood
of their own children on fire
with the flames of sinners,
with the glowing hatreds
mixed with the mute terror
of lonesome bitches? –

Every glance of the children,
glowing in wide open eyes,
is a vengeful poison –

Where are the mothers?

SHOESHINE BOYS

A.

Shoeshine boys at the corners,–
Shapes sculptured in high relief,
Painted with thousands of hands
by the city,
They have a greedy urge
to contemplate
the shapes of women
gliding by along the streets
from neck to heels
(Maybe from drinking too much
tequila, mescal and anise).
The glow in flashing eyes
drinks in
the attraction of girls' legs . . .

B.

Shoeshine boys at the corners,
who wear
hats like crown,
pressed down on their heads to their ears
the turned up brims cut
into zigzags,
In filthy clothes
themselves,–
they keep polishing
the shoes
of strangers,
A shiny bald spot–

on sunny, city pavements—
Their own feet, covered halfway,
Their toes sticking out of
torn shoes
like brown cigars—

C.

Shoeshine boys at the corners—
Aztec statues in stone—
at rest
beside city walls
on stony streets, that glow,
Crossed copper arms
on bent knees.
Shoeshine boys—
kneaded from clay—
They have
a home
next to the walls of the city street corners . . .

THE OLD WOMAN

*T*he old woman's head is like a wrinkled walnut;
Her yellow-grey hair like the mold of rotting moss–
Her hands–dry-sun browned, rotten bones–
hang down, like two halves of a broken board.

Her eyes, looking out from under the folds of skin on
    her forehead,
are like little red lanterns on nighttime street corners–
This little old woman knows–time has extinguished the desires,
that used to carry her off to faraway worlds somewhere.

If the wall is a shelter for dust and spiderwebs,
the countless graves for worms and flies,
then the city has also cast aside with its garbage
the body and the life of the forgotten old woman, clinging to
    the wall like a worm.

THE OLD MAN

*E*ighty, ninety, or a hundred maybe
That's his age, the old man at the gate;
I wouldn't even find it that surprising
if his face wasn't so full of sorrow.

He sits with outstretched hand
on the heated, glowing stones;
His overhanging white eyebrows
throw shadows across his eyes.

I contemplate the face of the old, grey man
Every wrinkle marking years of struggle . . .
How much misery
is he hiding in his thin, hollow chest? . . .

Why – I would ask –
was he unable to finish weaving his dreams of joy? . . .
How many roads has he measured
in his long, disasterous life? . . . .

How can I ask, when I tremble
at his crooked smile,
at his voice, begging so bitterly,
at his moaning, at his roaring.

And it seems, that I've known him for a long time
this old man with his hollow chest;
I count the wrinkles on his brown face;
Eighty, ninety, a hundred, maybe more . . .

AT DARK DOORS

I saw;–a woman, whose laugh was forced and painful,
making her way along a dark little street with dark doors,
with little red, square houses, painted in pale colors,
with beds in the bedroom for the prostitute daughters of poverty.

Who knows how many years of poverty lie hidden,
wrinkled under masks of joy on faces and eyelashes,
that have faded for pennies for powder and rice and tortillas.
I saw a woman like that. I heard her cold laughter.

With her glazed, sad eyes and lustful breasts,
who lives in a dark little room among the grey hovels,
with little sisters and an old mother too.

I have seen this woman fall
in a hoarse, dry coughing fit, smiling wanely,
to the cold ground like a bundle of rotten straw.

TUBERCULOSIS

*T*here is a woman dragging herself around—a TB microbe—
through the noisy, sunny streets of the swarming city;
Garments of rusty mold hang from her body,
dry mud baked into her feet.

There are those, such as she, who drag themselves around,
abandoned women, wrapped in filthy shawls,
in dirty, messy clothes, that are falling apart,
wiping the dirty streets with lousy rags.

And their dying eyes stare from emaciated faces,
They stretch their dry, wrinkled bones of hands—
They seat themselves along the walls like spots upon the stones.

They fry themselves in the mud on the hard stone pavement—
and the sickly poison spurts from them and spreads
black TB that goes on and on through generations, through eras.

A HUMAN BEING

*H*is shoulder against the yellowish wall,
his brownish body naked to the knees,
There's a human being under the burning sun—
indifferent to his exposed shame—

His fingers, pointing from his hand,
like dry little chicken feet—
His head like a picture on the wall,
browned by the tropical sun.

Each one of his eyes, sparkling with fervor
from the holes of his thin face.—
like a shiny worm crawling
in the hole of a dry tree trunk ....

Mouth open—from lip to lip—
Three widely spaced teeth—
his fingers, like chicken feet,
searching for something on the wall like a spider—

PEOPLE OF THE BACK STREETS

*T*he indifference of faintness pales out of everyone's eyes,
eyes as silent as old walls faded by the sun—
and hands with skin like brown bark on dried out twigs
They just hang down powerlessly, dangling from bodies.

And faces, wrinkling angrily at the world
Their fury falls on the grey emptiness of the streets—
People have provided themselves with bare, empty days,
like cowardly street dogs enjoying a bone in the garbage—

And every hour, that comes and goes, has been emptied
like the naked earth on the street of dust and holes—
The awful suffering along with a warmth that brings them joy,
warms up their insides and turns to hate—

HUNGER

Sharp eyes – dull stare –
and callused hands hang down –
Oh who will come to save the people now
from painful hunger, from bars of steel?

Hours die, like the flame of little lamps,
leaving emptiness in dark rooms;
and greyish days place their little grey imprints
upon the floor, walls, ceiling and every little corner.

And there are shadows lying around like flying ravens
and it seems like the beating and trembling of black wings,
And somewhere dogs dig in the garbage, howling
this angry, bitter forest wail.

The fields are full of corn, nourishing itself
The grains, uncut as yet, stand stiff and proud
and little children languish, cry and beg;
– a little piece of bread . . . a little piece of bread . . .

THERE IS A MAN WAILING A BITTER WAIL

*T*here is a man wailing a bitter wail,
as the sun bleeds a song—

Man!—
Your wailing won't do you any good—
If you can put up with it—
put up with
the day lying around in its death agony,
dogging your footsteps—

You want a day with a perpetual sun
because your fate—a gruesome wound—
lies on your days and weeks and years:

And your gaze falls on walls,
windows and street corners like a light signal,
cutting through quiet streets and glowing—

There is a man wailing a bitter wail,
as the sun bleeds a song—

CHURCHES

*T*he bells up in the steeples
still call the faithful to prayer, –
Every mute church
like an old graybeard turned to stone.

Their bodies faded by four centuries,
all full of wrinkles and grooves,
staring darkly through the gray spectacles of time
in amazement.

The calm pace of time
can't stamp out blind faith –
Petitioners still kneel and petition
at the open church doors.

And in every glance of the petitioners
there is a prayerful little flame, flaming away,
of holy Jesus religion.
hope and faith, as it did then.

When the armor-clad bronzed bodies,
in armor of iron and steel,
went striding through these streets here
with calm, measured strides.

The gruesome Spanish knights –
The ultra Catholic guards
of the holy church fathers
and monks all hooded and black.

And I still seem to hear the singing,
the choirs of pious nuns,
the Spanish inquisitors
with eyes that are glazed at prayer.
– Your light lights up all abysses,
  oh, holy Jesus on high –
  Your Name, so great and so holy,
  defiled by a servant of yours.

– Oh, purest one, Virgin Mary,
  begrudge him not, cleanse his soul
  Let the holy flames of the pyre
  wash away his sins . . .

And I still seem to see them leading
a victim through streets large and small,
the curses, the jokes and the laughter
of the pious crowd in his wake.

And I still see the faggots cracking
along with the bones and the ribs –
and the burned victim collapsing
with the word of God on his lips.

PERPETUO SOCORRO

A goddess, forever ready to help all those who seek help—
Why do you hang there so mutely,—
Are you really not ashamed of that shine in your eyes,
of that radiance emanating from your motionless face?—
I know—
You consider the people who praise you
fools—
victims of Christian love—

Then why is there so much hunger in those houses?—
Are the skeleton
children—
sinners—
The fathers, who beg,
The mothers, with wolverine eyes,
who lie
with their bodies nestled in the dirt?—

Oh, Goddess of Perpetual Help,
on a guilded, radiant throne,
I know—
You are merciful:—
Your heart has forgotten no one,
Fasting is virtuous—
Eating?—
That's for evildoers—

And all, who kneel here and pray
and expire from hunger
and languish for light—

Have you nothing for them?
Are you deaf to the
invalid's cry? –

Oh, goddess

You look great
May the evil eye shun you . . .
Your holy face
radiates satiety – well-being –

SUNNY SKY

Sunlight has been poured into the city,
On the roof a spreading golden ocean is making waves—
Every hour bounces by like a rubber ball
hitting the stones like string instrument sounds.

In the street we are like darkened abandoned beings
in an open crack in a cellar,
with night in our eyes and dark faces, facing the sun—the
    sparkling plate—

THERE'S A SUN HANGING

*T*here is a sparkling sun hanging over the city, torching away –
flinging off heated, burning pieces of itself –
The weary day moves along, staggering and staggering
like a drunk.

The stones on the street burn and the pavement heats up –
The dogs on the street drag themselves around with
    pricked-up ears,
People walk around with bare, steaming, sweating chests.

The small houses lie idly under bright sun covers,
Little grey points sparkle in the stifling hollow air, –
And the day, staggering exhausted, sneaks around lazily
with the help of a stick . . .

SALOON

*T*wo half doors swing when they open – two wide lips
    licking themselves –
A smell like the odor from an unwashed mouth hitting the narrow
    streets . . .
and inside, Juan and his pal slurping from the same bowl –
There is a round individual with a white apron on his chest – a
    barrel among the barrels –

A picture on the wall: a naked woman strumming a harp
    with fingers –
Juan standing there, a clay bowl in his dirty hand, his ardent
    gaze on the wall,
tells his pal: "Believe me, brother, no kidding,
I'm ready to exchange my blabbermouth of a wife for that frisky
    whore right this minute" –

MANANITAS

(Little Morning Songs)

Quiet call—
The weariness leaves my body,
Four in the morning.
A fiddlelike wail in the mute night,
A trembling sound—
Two guitars,
A man's voice singing . . .
I listen—
and every sound
of the engulfing tone
climbs, makes its way up to the balcony bars,
and her copper brown face appears
like a sorrowful heavenly praise—
From each
eye—
through brows, as though through a shadowy door—
a deep black sea bursts into sparkles,
making waves in the blue-dawn flame,
at every bend,
at every touch
of the trembling string sound—
And I in mute captivity,
wait quietly and long
in the dreamy call—
and the weariness leaves my body—

though my home is a distant strange land
I am wrapped in a sun-woven weave,
I feel comfortable with the shirt on my back,
I feel comfortable with the life that I lead . . .
Like an eagle in flight, on the hunt
speeding over giant mountains,
I too fly and I soar
bearing bright days with me
to gild the song that I sing.

RUINS REMIND US

*R*uins of temples
remind us
of the stride
and the swagger
of warriors on horses—
armored brutes,
who made
Indian blood flow
like rain,
who fertilized generous fields—
And Jesus on high
in his heavenly palace,
sent a bloody smile
through the smoke of the canon
to his crazed penitents and his servants,
who greedily nourished themselves
with the dried blood on the crosses.

Ruins of churches
remind us;—
of the holy Virgin
on thrones
of heavenly incest,
lit with love;
by people who lay
with red-hot wounds,
like sheep to the slaughter,
in the cold dark caves
of the church,
tied up

like sheaves–

The holes and cracks of the churches
that tell
of the dying of martyrs–
Indian ruins remind us:–
of cyclones,
that scattered
the peace and the faith of the Aztecs
like dust,
of women, of men and of children
in shackles
for the atonement
of nobody's sins–

And swords of iron and steel,
that cut up the bodies
of men and of women and children;–
and priests–
Those godly protectors–
who cut up their peace and their years
amid holy whispers,
like reapers
in fields reaping corn.

It's still around,
You can still feel the glow
of the sacred fury
of Spaniards –

Ruins of temples
remind us; –
how bloody
the Indian earth is.

CITY OF MUDPUDDLES

City of mudpuddles the size of rivers,
Tattered walls on low built shacks
Your grey, hungry people sneaking around on sidewalks
wrapped in rags.

And little children cry, grow pale and shudder,
lying around in stinking yards—
City, how I would like to run from you,
leaving no traces of my heavy steps.

So many generations have walked upon your body,
and you've grown even more cruel, ugly and black—
with poverty dancing through your crooked streets.

You've scattered pain on every wall here,
brought disaster upon forlorn homes

by now—there's a struggling victim in every one.

IT'S FREE

*I*t's free –
The glow
of sunlight on rags,
that hang from weary bodies
in filthy tatters
the right to stretch your limbs out
like a lonely dog beside the fence –

It's free
The dream of bread
and flowers,
of fields and trees and twigs;
Its free
to keep your mouth shut
when you feel the screams begin to rise.

The desolation creeping out of houses, –
a blind shadow –
leaving behind
the crying of children,
the sorrow of mother's,
the fathers' helpless worry
and long, dark moments –
The road to joy fenced off –

So what? –
The hunger that dries the blood,
is free –

*O*ut of the ruins of the old convent,
out of the earth, out of iron and stone,
I still hear the stifled cries,
the bitter wailing that comes
out of every corner and crack
crawling along the walls . . .

I seem to see an old capuchin monk
out of the old convent –
spreading his hands like a spider
and his scornful lips whisper;
"A man has profaned God" –

A man has been burned

Out of the cracks of the old convent –
The voice of a priest at prayer –
"The love of women – is sin –
Oh, God – man is so small" –

The priests themselves
violated those sinful bodies –

Out of the ruins of the old convent,
a shudder, a rustle, a call; –
"The body torn apart with pliers,
hands ripped from the trunk,
The children, the sister, the wife,
hands and feet cut up.
Bodies shackled in chains,
racked limb by limb,

Water dripping drop by drop,
boring holes in their heads" –

You can hear the walls whisper to this day
in the caves of the old convent –

TEOTIHUACAN

*Y*ou thousand year old Pyramids in your stony silence
among the silent flatlands and the hills, –
How many prayers, how many mystic praises
did a people at peace sing to you? –

I have absorbed your silence
I only know that centuries ago
a people removed from other peoples
sang the praises of unknown gods.

Perhaps you have the steps of my great great grandfather
   upon you
and my blood bears the heritage of a secret from afar, –
Do my origins lie buried beneath your stones
in their endless, timeless silence? –

Who were those marvelous giants, those strong men,
who laid the granite and the heavy stones? –
Older peoples have given birth to new ones,
Only the pyramids remain unchanged

You pyramids –
Were your builders Egyptians,
Phoenicians,
Jews, perhaps? –

I know, the holy Christian faith
of the Spanish Inquisition
besmirched Toltek's name
to scare the whole world with wild indian stories,
to rob
the quiet peace,

to erase
these nations from the earth–

Sun over the pyramids–
covering the eternal secret with your flames–
Out of the ruins of the old convent
shadows crawl–
A mass of thousands all told–
Body follows body, like a snake–

Heads, feet, hands
move separately–

POPOCATEPETL

*P*opo–
Body hardened to stone with fleece of snow,–
thousands of years scream from your body
in a silent scream–

At rose-blue dawn
the sun drapes your white head
in multicolored stripes
like ribbons.

Winds–
invisible monsters riding at a gallop–
dashing about upon you, howling as they plunder,–
whistling and singing the songs of faraway lands.

How many secrets
accumulated in the rush of generations
lie hidden in your depths?–
How many marks
recorded in blood
on every single stone?–

Popo, I want you to carry me on your body
like a stone,
Would you reveal
your wonders to my silence–

Popo–
Mysterious white giant–
The sun, threw a spear at you
in the dark moments toward evening,
all lit up–

Now I see,
long vanished generations
bleeding
from your spinal cord –

How many wanderers have trod on your white skin? –
How many glowing steps? –

Death
is pacing about at your ankles –
This cold, white wonder
blooming
on your back –

*Y*ou like to stop and look at the moldering carved doors
of shabby buildings, built centuries ago,
at every carving and stone sculpture of old monasteries,–
and every crack in the splitting walls tells you so many secrets.

You hold every head of stone dear, every manuscript, you love
    their shadows,
You like to fondle and cherish every bit of hieroglyphic.
From every stone the old primative tribes mutely sing
long forgotten symphonies more beautiful than Beethoven's Ninth.

You gaze upon them with such pleasure, you seem so close to
    everything here . . .
and the unknown joy, grief and fear of alien grandfathers is
    also yours;
Along paths overgrown with grass, Cuatemoc of the feathered head,
    the last hero of the Aztecs,
tells you tales of such bravery and such sacrifice.

And you imagine that you still can see the wild, glowing tongues
    of flame
upon the brown skin of the King's feet; armor clad
    shapes materialize;
Hernon Cortez, his flashing eyes driven by gold greed,
screams his commands at the victim; Tell me where you hid the
    gold you dog?–

And Huitzilopochtli–God of war–nourished by human blood,
Mute stone head–dull hard stare–
No longer can he still his hunger with the dripping blood and
    fluttering hearts in the stone pipes,

as he did in those crude times when one tribe savagely
    crushed another.

Anahuak is big and every idol has given you a sign,
The origins of all the tribes from the Navahos to the Mayans is
    not unknown to you—
I too would like to learn the secret of peace through the search
    for lost generations as you have,
not following those lost thousands of years as the bereaved
    follow funerals.

Are there others like you, quiet temperaments,
who collect little stones and pick up gems from vanished one upon
    a times?—
You have locked yourself in a temple of forgotten cultures
like a sunbeam lowering itself through the cracks of
    black valleys.

For you every shard of an old grey pot
is a holy talisman left by peoples of bygone days—
If only you could, you would hide from the world of today
and go back to the secret, distant past; body and soul.—

You are in touch with every little bit of something along these
    strange roads,
Bits of the heritage—moldy little stones, old monasteries—
Your childhood didn't come into being upon these flaming prairies
You've been seduced by wanderlust like me and like the others.

Anahuac—The name the conquerers used in Mexico.
Huitzilopochtli—A god to whom the Aztecs made human sacrifices.

CONTRASTS

City of palaces, you stone box,
surrounded by a hilly chain in the valley.
Your guts are full of the wildest of contrasts,
of misery, hunger and the joy of abundance.

Your asphalt streets are full of the rush
of speeding cars and trolleys;
but you also have back streets like piles of garbage,
where the day lies around in rags.

Your insides contain churches and convents
The houses are built of marble and stone;
There are people like worms on small dusty streets,
in little clay hovels–in holes of filth . . .

The little shacks there are built of clay bricks
covered with rusty tin roofs,–
A string and a rag–is a cradle for children . . .
shirts covering bodies–a sack in shreds–

In stone palaces behind locks of iron,
silk clings to female bodies,–
The wine that they drink is drawn from barrels
Their day to day joy bursts into drunken dancing.

On dirty little steps, next to brown containers,
The silk on their bodies–the glow of the sun;
Their wine is pulke–in little clay pots–
They drink down their poverty, warming their blood . . .

Oh, city of palaces, you carrier of misery! –
The weight on your shoulders has increased . . .
You have people, who sleep on soft beds and still more
asleep on the filthy ground . . .

pulke – A specifically Mexican alcoholic beverage.

rotting wood of old boards
and stolen typewriters,
hammers,
pincers,
files,
little beds
used and broken
rusty clock faces,
pots,
dozens of plates,
big and little shoes without soles,
half torn socks
and stained ties,
screws from old beds,
axles from wooden wheels,
tin coal bins,
people,
bars,
rags,
clothing
rot in the Tepito market.

His chest, bare and hollow,
His face full of inflammations,
His flattened, shaggy hair
on his flat, brown forehead—
There's a man, who sits beside the doors of strangers . . .
tears streaming down his cheeks, non-stop.
What can such a person lose?
And what can he still hope to find?—
Since nothing much remains
of his own grey life by now . . .

The hot sun glows upon his body,
burning his face for spite . . .

He sits beside the doors of strangers
with his rotting pile of rags . . .
cursing non-stop,
babbling strange, quiet words,
pressed against the hard wall,
drinking down his angry sorrow
with mescal and tequila . . .

There's a singer
in the middle of the market place,
his hat, with its loose straws,
pressed way down over his
sweating forehead.
That ardent voice of his is singing
the forest song of Mexico
He also sings about the prairies,
about a youthful senorita
Both his eyes—
sharp darts
sun heated,
pointing wildly from his
bronze carved face.
Her heart, beating at a gallop,
her fiery blood driven
throughout her brown body
heated by the wild, hot tropics—
She—cut up
her false brown bridegroom,
among the hills and the wild grasses,
with a flashing knife. . . .

The singer sings
and all around him—
little children,
men
and women
stand quietly,
black eyes devour
the sound of the singer's song,
Piously
they shake their heads and
sigh a prayer
and forget
their hunger
The body glows
in its wild burnings
The blood absorbs
the singer's song—

Flies buzz
in the mud—
Sticky grey pus . . .
And a drunk
staggers dully
like a nut . . .
And another—
exhausted by drink—
lies on a bed of garbage,
in the deepest sleep
constant snoring—
Mouths slurp
white pulche from mugs

in saloons
at the corners.

Mothers carry
little children on their backs
wrapped in cloths.
Thin little legs dangle
on their mothers' backs . . .
Sparkling, black eyes
stare rigidly
from emaciated
faces . . .

People sit on the stones
mute and bent
gnaw away at hard tortillas
with yellowish white teeth . . .
Trembling, frightened dogs
look for bones
in the garbage . . .
Gaze desolately
howl bitterly
in misery —
or hunger —

Young women
Black apples of their eyes stare boldly
under painted
brows . . .
Jet black
curled hair
decorated
with colorful combs,

Lips turning blue
painted red –
used up –
drawn arrogantly –
in misery –
or desire –

There's a cold sorrow
crawling around
on the grey sidewalks,
and from the sides
of walls enclosing every courtyard –
black holes
of doors –
stare –

People get themselves entangled, like balls of thread
next to arrangements of boards
where there are piles of tomatoes
full of hungry flies
and they're rotting . . .
Hoarse choruses rasp
in the motionless air, –
Dull sounds –
blend with
singing . . .
Sad,
desolate
horrors
float around . . .

And close by
there's a skinny person, staggering,
yelling and cursing wild curses:
–Oh, how glad I am to be
the lord and emperor of all the
wild poisons burning
in my heart . . .
Hey!
You, who have it so good, with your full bellies–
I'm your father–only I–
Daughters, sons of your mothers . . .
Why are you making faces? . . .
Why are you making them at me? . . .
Hey,
Cowards!–

I can lie down in the streets,
in the stinking garbage,
My miserable life
like a rotting corpse . . .
and make my bed
on cold hard stones
and lay
my skinny limbs down,
and put my head
on a "soft" pillow
of advertising posters . . .
Can you compare yourselves to me
and reach
the level
to which I have sunk? . . .
I can drink down

my suffering
with drinks,
that set the joy
in my breast aflame—
Daughters,
Sons of your mothers!—
You tell me
Who are your fathers?—

Dressed in rags,
in tattered shirts,
hollow naked
little stomachs—
Dirty, brownish children
jump around happily
and dance ...

A wrinkled
grey
old woman—
coughs and clears her throat—
sucking
the nauseating
juice of rotten oranges ...

There's a dead,
decaying dog
in the gutter ...

Hordes of flies
swarm
on his body ...
like a hive ...

Soon they all fly off
and hover,
fill the air with
putrid smells ...

Close by
a man is selling drinks ...
Refreshment for the heat ...
Bottled juice of tropic plants ...

People come—
lazy walkers—
Wipe their sweating faces,
Their woven sandals
squeak
on the hard and muddy stones,
drinking
Guzzling
from the bottles ...
Sipping sweetened yellow water
through big teeth ...

A pale Indian is sitting
on the ground,
beside piles of leaves,
and plants,
bits of twigs,
pieces of tree trunks,
and herbs ...
Sitting there in stubborn silence ...

Men arrive,
Old women
wrapped in shawls,

wearing aprons . . .
Girls come,
fellows too
with bronzed bodies
from the neighboring streets, –
They buy twigs,
bits of roots,
for all sorts of ailments . . .

For pain in their lungs,
for their heads
or for their kidneys . . .

Children guide
blind mothers,
blind fathers,
little children –
One is smaller than the other . . .
Little skinny hands stretching
toward the men,
toward the women.

Little children
drag themselves around Tepito
like experienced beggars:
"Look, my father's blind,

Can't you give an old, grey man
just one cold and dry
tortilla" . . .
The troubled heart of the old man weeps in silence –

He can't stand the begging
He can't listen to the voice of

the small boy—
How much longer will his heavy
feet drag themselves around in blindness? . . .
How much longer will
his evil fate drag him through darkness? . . .

And the people—
young
and old—
sunken cheeks—
every drop of blood drained from them
by starvation,
flesh consumed—
eyes
stare
blankly,
mute
and quiet—
They don't even have a bite
to eat
or a place to lay their heads—

Night arrives—the sorrow singer
wrapped up in a cloak—
Night arrives—the shadow jumper
Playing an old harp:

Strumming with his long black fingers
on the tuneful strings,—

Tunes leap
and fall apart
upon the dark black holes,

upon the stones,
upon the doors
of the houses –

And the bitter gloomy waves
float away
and scatter
into the corners of the doorways,
where people huddle
reveling
in their bitter poverty –
their pain laughing
in their grim, malicious stares –

Battered walls,
Paneless windows,
The old, grey
church
stands in the rotting filth
within, a silent pious
prayer
behind closed doors –
the silence
is so mute.
like the silence
of a dead man –
Beside the church –
like shadows
silent slinkers
slink
picking
other people's refuse,

rotten fruit
in the garbage —

And a woman
just like carrion,
sores cover
her bare breasts
and exposed brown body,
her messy black tufts of hair
in her wild, flaming eyes —
She lies stretched
beside the old doors of the church —
and a clenched fist
beats
her hollow chest
and she has a coughing fit:
— Nobody will touch me here —
She screams, laughing
Not even the watchman
with his stick —
The hell with the whole world,
I'm the queen here! —

Like a hard, stiff doll,
Tense as an instrument string,
There's a drunk at the gate,
Saliva pouring through his teeth
And he grumbles,
all bunched up like a sack,
He collapses on the ground
and falls asleep . . .

Bare chest and shoulders
Straight ahead to meet the darkness,
Shaky movements—
a yelling, cursing man walks by,
Savagery flashes from his eyes
Words pour from his broad mouth:
—Who needs a home—a wife and child?—
I don't need anybody—
My wife—that filthy bitch—found someone else
Damn her to hell—

Pressed against walls"
at black corners
brown hands
lift coffee cups
to lips.

And on stairs
small heads
on stones
children lie—
bags of bones—
huddling in a cold shudder
and they all bunch up together—

And they dream about a mother,
about beds
made on mattresses
and pants that have no patches—
They feel warm:
There's a fire in the heater,
Steam rises from the pots—
what a great fine miracle . . .

Near the children
There's a man playing guitar, –
Sad sounds jump
out of the tender string shudder,
He sings along
Another helps him
and a third one–
and all three sing
tranquil village songs together
Their black eyes flame
under wide brimmed hats
and they guzzle
white liquor from clay pitchers.

And the sky draped in black
wraps the houses up in shawls
His red eyes gaze
at little streets full of holes,
at those who stagger as they stride,
wrapped in many colored cloths.

Walkers
walk–
lazy mares–
dragging heavy feet
over the stones–

And there's this little guy–
all skin and bone
and another guy,
who's with him,
like a short fat little barrel,
with his bare, brown chest,

and they both go dragging themselves around the
    market booths
and their steps are so tranquil,
and their thoughts are so secret,
They look around so tensely
with such a distraught gaze—
No one's coming—

And the guy all skin and bone
says to the other guy—
the barrel:
—Hey, you wild devil, you jackass
Here's the iron,
Here's the hammer
Dumbbell—
Okay, let's see what you can do—
Tear off the little lock
.I'll look out . . .

The smoldering gaze
of the skinny one
scans the deserted sadness of the night.

He looks—
and sees—
no one coming,
no one coming,
There's not a fly buzzing in the air,
There's no watchman at the corner.

The fat one starts
breaking the boards
and the rotten wood just splits
and the door

opens wide.
The two of them just stand there
gaping—wide-eyed—
at the emptiness
inside the booth . . .

Black night—
A malevolent spirit
covers the night with black cloths.
Wild flashes
sparkle
in four eyes.
as though looking through dark glasses . . .
teeth grind
in fury . . .

And the fat guy fumes and yells
His brown face starts getting paler,
His mouth opens showing teeth,
He spits on the stones in fury.
He sharpens his wild flaming gaze
at the man all skin and bone.
—Damn it, damn your mother!
You said there was a whole fortune
locked up in this booth
and that we would have enough
to eat and drink for years and years . . .
that we could both forget what hunger
is like for a long long time . . .

The thin guy stands there
mute and rigid
Not a word

He doesn't move an inch
and his lips twitch:
His fearful gaze
falls on the fat one
His hands clench ...

And the fat guy grabs the hammer,
slams the thin guy on the head: –
– Take that, stupid,
This is the last time you fool me ...

The thin man, all skin and bone,
just fell down upon the stones
red eyes tearing,
writhing as he roared
He was crawling on all fours
and he took a sharpened dart
from his pocket,
stuck it into
his friend's fat belly
with his stiffened fist:
There you go – Keep my knife here ...

And the night – the sorrow singer –
tuned the old harp
with long black fingers –

And then, roaring in their hunger,
whole crowds of dogs appeared and howled –
barking as they jumped around
and started licking
the red spots on the stones
with stretched tongues –

Tepito
Marvel fostered from dark sorrow,
Swollen body of bursting wounds . . .
Forever lurking in seething anger
The City of Palaces facing your body.

The stone monster, with glowing eyes,
with teeth of steel, that bite and devour,
and suck your heart's blood – Tepito –
degraded misery in mute euphoria . . .

Your people here – rigid statues –
with bronzed bodies, as though forged from copper:
Lazily they drag the dark hours,
that grow rigid as they, on your back – Tepito . . .

And the sun fries your dark mud,
that lies like a sore, on the stone sidewalks . . .
and sickness erupts here – that black tuberculosis,
from thin figures that are mute and grow rigid.

Is there someone who will ask these quiet people,
why such joy amid such bitter poverty?,
And who will even dare to think
that joy can run wild in a hollow chest . . .

The sky, hanging over the market of Tepito,
is a grey cover on the body of a corpse . . .
The booths – a black, rotting deathbed
in a mute graveyard of desolate poverty . . .

MEXICAN NIGHTS

A.

On such cold,
fearful dead
black nights,
when the mute city stiffens –
into a dark stiffness, –
Pale slaves of hunger
creep around –
and softly make their way
through streets that have seen better days
Children of a moment of love –
look for a night's lodging
beside a hard, cold wall,
to huddle
weary limbs –
Skin stretched on bone,
desiccated by starvation, –
On the stones
with street dogs . . .

B.

And in noisy salons
and in torrid cabarets,
the wild sounds
of flute and drum and jazz orchestras
leap about
and tear the air to pieces.
and feet stamp, step
to the loud rhythm

of fox trot music din,
as though someone were after them
driven by devilish impulses
in a sea of hot breath –
and the couples turn
arms closely wrapped around each other,
bodies pressed closely
in convulsions of lust.

C.

And on the streets, as darkness falls,
and at the corners, drenched in rain,
beside lanterns sparkling through the grey,
they sneak around,
with sorrow smiles,
with cynical death laughter,
in a lonesome confiding,
Pale women
in makeup masks
and they're waiting
for a man,
in order to bestow
burned out death lust on him
upon a torrid whore's bed
for a piece of bread and powder . . .

D.

And at half-lit windows,
when the weary night rests,
shadows push
against the panes
Whole crowds of pale shadows

of the people
never born into this world
from all the hot seed
time spilled
in her wild and greedy lust ...
And they float about, these shadows,
in the wild and stormy winds,
screaming:
—We need the sunlight of the real worlds,
  We need breath and we need motion!
  Our own flesh and blood condemned us
  to a death before our birth.
  Pale shadows—we are sinking
  in oblivion's abyss ...

MIDNIGHT

*M*idnight.
Night–the angry
shadow maker–
wraps itself around the houses.
and frightened
bells
ring,
sounds
lament
Screams
sing songs
at the corners . . .
Whom will they carry
through the blind night to the graveyard?
Is someone mourning a lost loved one?–
it's even more amazing!–

Children singing
in the filth
bedded down on paper
beside the closed doors of stores . . .

City–
You bed of stone–
Reveal your secret,–
It's midnight–

NIGHT

Evening has wrinkled its dark face
into flabby late hour grimaces like a devil—
The reflection of the lanterns has Painted
loose bits from spools of white thread on the streets.

A cool silent hour arrives in the land where night reigns
The little houses sit there all bunched up like old men;
and it seems that night is winding out of the summits of
     the hills
like unfolded, bunched up shadows of ragged sheets—

STARS

These are no streets where people wend their way
but deep split valleys—
The body of the city is not swollen
with houses of granite and stone,—
There are long long lines of ancient skeletons
with dry bare bones.

There is no sky over the broad city,
no gayly twinkling stars,—
The grey evening
climbed a ladder before dying
dipped its paint brush in red paint
and splattered some on a black sheet—

SLEEPING STREETS

*M*ute houses–dark, grey shapes–
jutting out of the nightliness in stony silence.
The steps of the night people rise like violin sounds
They lift themselves and climb, leaving no traces.

And thin-skinny lanterns like forlorn figures,
look into the darkness with a single red eye;
sorrowing in silence as though bewailing a corpse,
shuddering with sleepy, squinting, cataract eyes.

Here and there a little guy stumbling along
hits a wall in his drunken meandering,
Somewhere a car sounds off with mean, loud grumbling.

The wild lustful kidding of a foxtrot
breaks through the open windows of blue cabarets,
waking the quiet night lying on black streets.

EVERY NIGHT

Every night–
As I walk down the street,
where I live,–
I see this person
with hollow black eyes
like night itself:
and a kind of weeping–
a wavelike moan
flows
through his yellow teeth.

I stop
hand leaning
against the
grey wall
thinking:
What can he want?–
Try asking him–
His eyes
stare fixedly
into the black emptiness
from his heart–emptied
by the night.–

A MAN WHO HAS LOST HIS JOY

*T*here is a man walking down the street unaware of his own
   heavy steps
playing out some mute secret upon the mute stones;
A man who has lost his joy has lost God too,
trickling through his blood in every singing limb—

The hardened soles of his feet—like the soles of shoes—
Dirty, lazily, wearily, they plod along the streets
His eyes stare blankly into the motionless emptiness
of the dark, mean night, singing a dark song.

His swarthy, pock-marked face is a prototype
of an Aztec statue wrought in stone—
A kind of mute lament comes rolling from his throat,
straining through the yellow strainer of his teeth.

His hands hang down from his shoulders like two pieces of wood,
His fingers, long rusty scraps of cast metal,
that stifled his gruesome scream long long ago,
a scream, tearing from his breast, like terror in the evil night—

The world stretches far and wide but this man feels hemmed in
   and small,
although he has a blue roof with shining jewels above him—
He doesn't feel the hunger drying out his throat,—
He revels in his own grief like a dog with a dry bone—

A man who scorns and laughs away every earthly threat,
as the wind laughs at the wanderer in the bleak desert,
His body feels the joy of rest on the cold, hard sidewalk,
Like a child asleep at its mother's white breast.

A man walking down the street, unaware of his own
    heavy steps
playing out some mute secret upon the mute stones–
The blood within him is quiet, every limb turned to stone–
A man, who has lost his joy, has lost God too–

A LODGING FOR THE NIGHT

I.

I have seen: – A man standing at the corner, trembling,
gazing down dark streets with the eyes of the lost,
his lips drawn, his face deathly pale,
estranged from his own life and split into splinters.

A dog with a twisted neck and bitter eyes,
trembling with fear, like a hare at the shot of a hunter,
Man and dog stood at the wall with no place to lie down
on the open street with the rain painfully storming.

I have seen: – a hand tearing posters off the wall,
and putting them down on the cold, muddy sidewalk of stone:
Man and dog huddled together on paper pillows . . .

And both dreamed – of gnawing discarded bones
from the garbage can there, in cloudy grey lantern light –
A dream of the starving on cold, muddy stones . . .

II.

Night is grey in the city, like burned out coal,
after the day, pulsating with life, gives up the ghost.
Police whistles – lazy and sad
go on and on, from corner to corner, like dull spiderwebs.

And way out there, beyond the city, upon grey dust and stone
there the night strides over sleeping poverty
and lays a bony hand on the dark hovels, –
There skinny dogs bark with dull cries . . .

And somewhere a man is tearing posters off the wall,
to serve as a cover on the raw, hard stones.
Such grey, shuffling shadows are everywhere,

looking for a threshold at a closed door . . .
It's every man for himself; thin, weary bodies,
huddled with their dogs on cold sidewalks . . .

WHEN A LONESOME DOG

When a lonesome dog, shivering at a cold, hard threshold,
with that way of barking, mouth upward, wolfish howl—
and night lies in such mute silence, in fearful horror,
that rises right up to the black sky with its sparkling beads.—

At that time every hour of the night comes to a motionless,
    petrified halt
and heavy darkness spreads itself—unyielding rigid—
The whistling of police whistles is carried along by wind,
that rolls into the hollow emptiness of every door—

And inside there are people lying like hunched up little sacks,
and it seems that every one of them is a rolled up mole—
They enjoy life in their reality of pain and scorn,
that black fate has sown upon their desert years—

And every day—a rusty ring of a long heavy chain,
woven around the rotting body of half the city—

AMOR

The bed—the bare damp earth—for two to sleep:
For him—a negative of a human form—and for his wife;
Their heated brown bodies absorb
the dampness mixed with the smell of old straw—

The wind rocks the door, banging like the tick tock of a clock,
The cool air—a cover for their glowing bodies—
What does a man like that need, who has his own wife beside him,
to share moments of joy in a common bed? . . .

What does he care about the screaming and lamenting of the cold
wind,
with black night covering him as a mother covers a child?—
Even if the wind were tearing pieces of his house away—
with joy clinging so closely to his aching body—

The night has hammered torrid hours upon his body
Even bleak fate has no hold on him—

BLACK ASPHALT

*B*lack asphalt –
Mattresses
of stone streets spread
in the City of Palaces, –

Do tell, how many children
with thin little bodies
lie sleeping
cuddling their dogs? . . .

Do tell, how many
abandoned beings
are to be found
on your hard, mute stones?

And how many
betrayed women
doing lustful deeds
with sin in their bones? –

You stones,
bear witness, –
Why the silence – why won't you speak? –
Are people without beds
something to be happy about?

Oh, tell me, to whom
lone women
should be ashamed
to trust their bodies,

that have the gift
of fire in their blood?–
Even lust is precious
to people who glitter–

why the silence, you mute ones
in the terror the night brings
and you gaze as they come,
no bread–no homes–

emaciated forms–
desolate gazes–
their fingers scrabbling
through tin garbage cans? . . .

Does it make sense that they,
who creep like worms,
one by one,
without homes, without anyone,
should find nothing
in your guts?–

Black asphalt,–
Can it be that the night has hidden a treasure in you? . . .

PEOPLE KNOW

*F*ields are full of blossoms, granaries are bursting,
but it seems that luck has come too late for people –

Their own work rots and fades – hammered shut in granaries
and poverty – a band on chests – clings to them – keeps clinging.

The sky throws down the gold of plenty and wraps it up in bundles –
Should I bless this bright and sun drenched day? –

All things brighten and warm up, making life seem dearer,
There's lots of gold out in the fields but no bread in the houses . . .

When the day, a miser, cries and wails with golden tears –
People know the rye is rotting, hammered shut in the granaries –

When the sun makes magic through her eyebrows like a witch,
People know the rotting bread in the granaries is for no one –

MEXICAN ROADS

*P*rairies and more prairies—prairies of distant hills,
draped in blue transparent scarves
like naked women in trailing garments of tulle
upon sunny fields with golden waves—

Fields and more fields upon hilly skins
with ripe sugar cane rising stiffly,
like sunny lit wicks of yellow,
that burn and burn and never burn out—

Roads and more roads—roads of crooked hills,
My steps become entangled in you,
I have encountered a summer silence upon you—
caressing and warming—burning red hot.

Trees and more trees—like hands
reaching toward the golden horizon in prayerful imploring—
I have drawn in your quiet deeply
My home in a strange land becomes near and dear to me.

PRAIRIES

*H*ere the sun burns and blazes on the prairie
Day has fallen into the glowing sphere—
The hours, like hooded nuns,
move slowly—

Indians shuffle along, together with their donkeys,
their bodies wrapped in brown shawls—
the sand hills come to a point like old men's heads
with yellowish bald spots—

A car from some place—a guest who is a stranger
scatters the dust right up to the blue cover of the skies—
The Prairies, like wanderers in open shirts,
lie dozing—

BRIGHT DAYS

*B*eneath the tropical sun I like to cling to
the hot brown earth, in the warmth of sunrays –
Let my misery disintegrate into dust and splinters
so that my heart's joy sings and runs wild.

I feel close to the sunny land, I feel that it is my land
with its hilly fields, woodlands and grasses –
I left my grey youth behind me somewhere
in the distant past upon totally alien roads.

And although I wasn't born and raised here –
I have sunny days here – for me the morning light
and I have lost my sadness somewhere.

I have cleansed myself the fire of suns,
choked my sorrow with sunny fingers,
and found my happiness in the sunny land.

FIELDS

So much quiet—
hard as steel patience
upon hilly roads,
upon swollen, crooked
earth.

Brownish Indians
plough the fields:
their black
eyes blazing
and mute.

Greyish oxen
pull the plough
upon sunny fields,
where day is glowing
and burns.

Corn will rise quietly,
like village singing,
upon dozing fields,
known to me
for quite a while.

GOLDEN SHEAVES

*G*olden sheaves lie in the silver valley,
Green brightness rises from the abundant flatland,
and the sun washes the day in molten steel
and paints the branches on the trees in yellow.

The surrounding hills turn bright, bright blue—
Their peaks lean toward the gold horizon.
how you want to be in touch with yourself
and close to happiness on such a glowing day . . .

And the silence, a warm caressing veil,
wraps my soul in a sunny garment,
Life itself is worth a zero compared to
all the joy in a split second of happiness . . .

ETERNAL SPRING

*T*he eternal spring, that greens in this tropical land here,
makes a smooth, green velvet bed for the crooked hilly earth, –
and you need an eye like a pointed telescope
to find a withered tree here.

How I would like to see one of those snowy winters
Snowflakes falling, like bits of wool from a shorn sheep,
and the funereal wail of blizzards chasing
a frozen day.

I still would like to live to see the little children
pelting each other with great, big snowballs,
and though spring is eternal here and everything is marvelous,
I'd like to wander.

IN THE VILLAGE

*G*rey swollen earth –
Blue hills in green valleys
Nuts with wrinkled shells
scattered among the flowers.

Trees twine and tangle –
softly stroking horizons,
as though someone near and dear
was embracing them.

Low little hovels,
fall apart on uneven ground,
like little boats upon the waves
swimming away in a sun sea.

And Indians drag themselves wearily
up the hills like up the stairs,
and seem to stick to
the deep cracks in the hills.

Evening fails on trees and grasses,
Shadows spread and dissolve,
and a breeze rises and blows
with cold breath.

Day puts on a veil
and evening puts out the fire . . .
the wind, the screamer, gets mad
because the day is hiding.

TENANGO DEL VALLE

*T*he speeding car—
A roadside hill,
Little Indian houses—arranged at the top—
like blisters on the hunchback
of a man lying on his stomach—

A howling wind over the road—
A wildly galloping cowboy—
and high over hilly meadows
little lights go on and flicker—

Little windows sparkle—

The night—
A little old lady with a kerchief on her head
is cupping—
a sick body—

cupping—Applying cupping glasses formerly used by physicians to draw
blood to the skin as a remedy for various maladies.

A SUNLESS DAY

*T*he hills are sitting all bunched up like sick people,
hidden right up to their heads in woolen kerchiefs—
Little oak stumps stick out of the earth
like the small swollen bellies of starving children—

The day—a doctor—with this greyish beard,
lines up every hour—like medicine jars—
The clouds—wrinkled, whitish little sheets—
cover the little hills—the hospital cots—

A doctor—the day—with a beard so grey,
displays every hour—medicine bottles—
The clouds—crumpled-up, whitish sheets—
cover the hills—hospital beds—

BY THE DAY'S ABYSS

By the day's abyss, I like Just to stand and wait
for the hours, like silver bells, to come and meet me;
I like just to stand and look at mountain roads,
and at wagon-wheels that rattle across hard paving.

I like the slow shuffling of donkeys–the size of greyhounds–
that move in long files, with timber on their backs;
Indians, with pots on their shoulders, with innocent glances
of flashing eyes from haggard, coppery faces.

I like the scattering of sunny dots on peaks
of giant mountains, like heads of monstrous beasts:
from them, like pointed ears, stick out the mescal-thorns.

I like the broiled earth-body in the glowing heatwave–
like a bluish wavy swirl in a motionless sea.
I like to stand and wait on the mountain roads.

WRAP YOURSELVES AROUND ME

*W*rap yourselves around me, cool, still, greyish twilights;
I've been baking under the hot sun all day,
With tranquil steps I come to you exhausted.
Let me rest in your shadow now
after a long, lanquid day.

Wrap yourselves around me, cool, still, greyish twilights;
I don't know who put my heart's joy under lock and key,–
It is quivering, trying to tear itself from my faint heart.
The face of the day is spattered with blood–
I don't know who slaughtered the bright day . . .

Wrap yourselves around me, cool, still, greyish twilights,
Wrap me up in your grey mantle;
Think of me as a shadow too;
I want to confide in your darkness with all my heart,
I want to forget this day, to think of other days.

DYING DAY

*T*he weary day dozing toward evening
fades,
dies, –
and gloomy seconds, grey shadows,
spread . . .

And on the rim of heaven the sun's hand
draws,
paints
blossoms
in bloody dying reds and blues . . .

The cool fingers of the sad wind
tear,
pick at
the hours, like trembling
mandolin strings –

The mean night – a dark and quiet
ghost –
shoves
the deceased day, in its black casket,
into the grave . . .

EVENING ON THE PRAIRIE

*L*ate hours
kindle
bloody red flames—
Evening winds
glow—

Grey clouds—donkey herds—
go on and on

and fade
and vanish
into the black valleys somewhere.

Prairies doze—
Green barrel cacti
like petrified shapes,
playing, playing ballads
with stiff spread fingers
on the strings
of the bloody guitar
the sun has painted
in the heavens—

SUNLAND

*I*n my wandering through tropical prairies
I want to become a blowing breeze
and drink the joy of trees and grasses
from sunny goatskins.

I want to become a sunbeam
cuddling the hills like children,–
at night a star in the sky–
an eye, observing black marvels–

On Sunland, unlike other countries
with their frosty days on the road,
I'm a wanderer here a stranger–
The gold of your sun is my fortune.

I wasn't born on your body.
but I feel so much part of it all–
I want to be a star in your heaven–
A silent perceiving eye–

TIME IS A MILLER

*F*ields drenched
in silver suns,
and crooked forest-covered hills
clad in eternal green —
On, tell me, where can I
find my joy here,
My joy that lost its way
and I don't know where it went.

My joy that I have sought
in kind of crooked valleys,
on the prairies, in the cities
and on roads and trails . . .
Time is a miller,
a miller who ground up,
my golden joy
in the course of days.

I've left my white childhood
far far behind me
somewhere in Poland
on the wide, flat Polish plains
Once upon a time I heard
my father tell a story
about some rider
and his golden horse . . .

The years have gone by
and I am the rider
My horse is black

and his head is raised.
The road to the joys
of this world is a long one—
My horse has collapsed
at a gallop.

Through cities and fields,
through valleys and hills
I traveled alone
There was no one around
because time is a miller,
a miller who ground up,
my golden joy
into sand, into dust . . .

DEFINITIONS OF MEXICAN TERMINOLOGY

A

Anahuac–Mexican name for the Spanish conquest.
anapre–A square box, which serves poor Mexicans as a kitchen.
anise–Sweet liqueur.
Aztecs–A warlike Indian tribe in Central Mexico.

B

boleros–Shoeshine boys.

C

canios–Sugar cane.
cantinas–Saloons.
Capuchin–A Franciscan monk.
Charros–A famous Mexican rider and steer roper.
Charro hats–An ornamented, broad-brimmed hat made of
  cloth.
City of Palaces–Pseudonym for the capital of Mexico.
cobijas–Scarves.
códices–Historical manuscripts regarding antiquities.
convento–church.
Cuautemoc–Last king of the Aztecs.

D

Desierto de los Leones–Area near the capital, where there is a
  temple of the Spanish Inquisition.

G

gachupinas–Term of abuse for the Spaniards.

H

Hernan Cortez–The conqueror of Mexico.

Huaraches–Sandals worn by the ancient Aztecs. The Indians still wear them.

Huaichilipotchtli–A god, to whom the Aztecs made human sacrifices; their prisoners of war, whose hearts were cut out.

I

idolos–Idols.

J

jacalas–Huts.

jarros–Clay pitchers.

M

mageas–Thorny plants, from which mescal as well as pulje are extracted.

maize–Corn.

mananitas–Early morning songs, which are played for friends and sweethearts.

marijuana–A drug.

Mayans–An Indian tribe in the Yucatan Peninsula (Mexico) and Guatemala.

mescal–Mexican whiskey.

N

Nahoas–A race, that once existed in South America.

P

perpetuo socorro–Goddess of eternal help.

petatos–Mats spread on the ground, on which poor Mexicans sleep.

Popo–Abbreviation of Popocatapetl.

Popocatapetl–A famous volcano in Mexico always covered with snow. "Black man."

puestos–Booths at a market place.

pulke–A specifically Mexican intoxicating beverage.

pulkeria–A saloon, where pulke is sold.

Purisima Virgen Maria–Most pure Holy Virgin Mary.

R

rebozos–Women's shawls.

S

serapes–Multicolored woolen scarves, worn instead of coats.

sentimiento–Mood–A peculiar mixture of various feelings, such as sadness, joy, kindness, ferocity, etc. Sentimento is not the well known "sentiment".

señorita–Miss.

T

tamales–Mexican dish made of corn flour.

tequila–Mexican whiskey.

Tenango del Valle–Name of a Mexican village.

Teotihuacan–An area, where there are pyramids dedicated to the sun and the moon.

tepache–A beverage made of tropical fruits.

Tepito–The poorest, filthiest neighborhood in the capital.

Toltecs–An Indian tribe.

Tunas–Cactus fruits.

tortieria–A bakery, where tortillas are baked.

tortilla–Flat roll made of corn.

tostón–A coin worth fifty centavos.

V

Virgen–Holy Virgin.

*One thousand copies
have been printed from Minion type at the
Stinehour Press in Lunenburg, Vermont.
Designed by Jerry Kelly.*

✳